Purification in Queens

Kristalyn Gill

Fernwood
PRESS

Purification in Queens

©2024 by Kristalyn Gill

Fernwood Press
Newberg, Oregon
www.fernwoodpress.com

All rights reserved. No part may be reproduced
for any commercial purpose by any method without
permission in writing from the copyright holder.

Printed in the United States of America

Page design: Mareesa Fawver Moss
Cover art: Nathanael Myers
Author photo: Mike Esperanza

ISBN 978-1-59498-150-0

Also by Kristalyn Gill:

she was familiar with wars
The Breakup Club: A Collective of Mishaps and Falling Aparts
The Shape of You

In her scintillating poetry collection, Kristalyn Gill strips away the priestly garments of Catholicism to expose the emptiness within. At once a confession and an indictment, *Purification in Queens* pulls religious skeletons out of the closet to make room for tender hearts that want to know God. With incisive clarity, Kristalyn investigates her understanding of family, faith, and womanhood, and explores how God comes to us in the gritty, uncomfortable parts of life. This collection is for anyone who wants God in a real way, who is tired of empty words, and who is on the quest for spiritual substance.

—ELIZABETH MOORE
co-author of *Liturgies for Hope*

Kristalyn Gill's *Purification in Queens* successfully grapples with the intricacies of religiosity and girlhood. It is a celebration of reclaiming femininity and faith. It is a transparent and honest manifesto of the complexities of living in a body. It is an ongoing game of Rock, Paper, Scissors when it comes to processing a nonlinear relationship with God. Gill's imagery throughout is so striking, you won't be able to put her book down.

—MAYA WILLIAMS
poet laureate of Portland, Maine, 2021–24

Poetry experts, lovers of words, and anyone who can appreciate a good rhyme scheme will find themselves sucked into the cathartic, cleansing cry that is *Purification in Queens*. Gill's words are the good kind of pain. They're a balm for the soul to those who have found both hurt and healing in faith—she has masterfully woven a story about absurd femininity, daughterhood, and even death. You will be undone by this book, and you'll come back to it again and again.

—HANNAH OH
assistant shopping editor at *Cosmopolitan*

Kristalyn's writing is cerebral yet grounded, unflinching but compassionate, clever but truthful. *Purification in Queens* delves into the hypocrisy of false religion, the wrestling match of real faith, the experience of womanhood, and the wounds of childhood with artfully crafted poems that are both bracing and comforting in their honesty. This book is refreshing for the heart and the mind.

—SARAH JANE SOUTHER
founder of Unfortunately, I Love You

Like its title promises, *Purification in Queens* dexterously and casually knits the sacred with the profane and the spiritual with the mundane. Gill's emotionally charged poems paint God, parenthood, death, city buses, and the human body with the same vivid brush—and they're better for it.

—CHLOE SARBIB
television writer, director, and editor

This poetry book is a companion for anyone who has danced themselves out of certainty into the open air of curiosity. Kristalyn Gill scrutinizes high-control ideologies and the expectations for women within those worlds ("I am a refugee within my ribs"). She shares the wonder of exploring things that were once off-limits ("They didn't tell us how kissing/ is just whispering *I'm not going anywhere*/ into someone else's wounds) and delights in the comfort of newly gained freedom ("Start to bury myself in curiosity,/ to cover myself with a question mark/ and call it home"). Gill says, "I believe in the weight of an unread book in your palm," and I believe that this is a book you should read after you've enjoyed its beautiful weight in your palm.

—JOANN RENEE BOSWELL
author of *Meta-Verse!: It's going to be interesting to see how yesterday goes*

?

For my fellow souls who bury themselves
beneath a question mark
and call it home.

*To what
will you look for help
if you will not look to that
which is stronger than yourself?*

—C.S. Lewis

CONTENTS

the book 12
IN THE BEGINNING WAS THE WORD 15
   the great perhaps 17
   you are what you eat 18
SHEEP IN THE MIDST OF WOLVES 19
   Confraternity's Resuscitation 21
   genu(ine re)flection 22
   the easter bunny and Jesus 23
   purgatory 24
   jump 25
   the burning man 27
   the witches brew 28
   it's not about the nail 30
   Purification in Queens 31
   Ashes and Asics 32
   have you ever 33
   four valuable lessons from a church-girl 34
   pennies from heaven 35
   popcorn prayer circles: a tragedy 36

SHE CAN LAUGH AT THE DAYS TO COME 39
- my femininity is that kind of girl 41
- little bean 44
- bless your heart, do your part 45
- a woman's place 46
- Rosie, just Rosie 48
- the gloaming 49
- An Ode to my Cervix 50
- The All-American Girl is 28 days old 51
- private school p*ssy 53
- imago d(e)issent 55
- parked in the driveway of a house where I do not live 56
- slits and ladders 57
- you can have it all (but not everything) 58

HONOR YOUR FATHER AND MOTHER 59
- Mother, may I? 61
- the hummingbird and the meadowlark 65
- one can of Canada Dry with a neon pink straw 68
- she only grows near water 70
- switchblade 71
- gone girl and what would've been her eulogy 72
- coal for Christmas 76
- midnight among the masses 78
- La Cara Norte 79
- surrogacy 80
- a man of your word 81
- too many fathers 82

SHE WHO HAS EARS, LET HER HEAR 83
- better, richer, fuller 85
- the swan song turned to stone 86
- the hill he dies on 87
- casual morbidity 89
- is this what they call depression? 90

salvation through repetition 91
squall—a localized storm, a loud cry 92
the day the moon fell 93
speed dial 95

BLESSED ARE THOSE WHO MOURN 97
  slipstream 99
  pulp fiction 100
  drunk on rejection 102
  a life worth dying for 103
  new age apocrypha 104
  nights like these 105
  how are you? 106
  food poisoning 107
  clothespin 108
  Icarus 109
  incandescent autumn 110

THE VALLEY OF THE SHADOW OF DEATH 111
  a list of things that haven't managed to kill me (yet) 113
  the realities of death: an exhaustive list 115
  supposed thoughtcrimes that
      leave Winston gagging in his sleep 116
  despite all things, a profession of faith 118
  the last, unforgettable line of a nonexistent story 119

Notes 121
Acknowledgments 123
About the Author 127
Title Index 129
First Line Index 133

the book

is me telling you, dear reader,
how I never feel enough

it's a journey to find certain words for certain conversations
it's a time capsule
it's also a lie

it's a secret
it's a story I've never heard
it's a myth and a mirror
it's a celebration of alliteration and long titles
it's faithfulness
it's fabrication
it's wrestling with my mid-twenties
it's a worldwide pandemic
it's marriage
it's womanhood
it's the interrogation of womanhood
it's breakups and births and burials

it's my evolution from silence into speech
it's enthusiasm on a not-so-empty page
it's hungry words gasping for air (and attention)
it's verbs eager to be wrapped in ink

it's the smell and the stench of home
it's the bullet hole of an apology I haven't received (yet)
it's the loose kite of all the love I haven't given (yet)

it's a book
it's a life
it's poetry pocket change
it's a paperweight
it's a deposit of your time you will never get back

it was mine
and now it's yours

so, thank you

IN THE BEGINNING WAS THE WORD

and the word was with God
and the word was God
and the word was
and the God
and the God was
and the God was with

the great perhaps

I am the restless peeling,
the gunshot of a body chewing on withered figs,
the copper bandage before a waterfall.

Rock, paper, schism.
Gash.

Like muscle memory,
my name clings to my mother's tongue.

I may not have changed the world,
but I was a busy existence.

Perhaps all skin feels like it is merely in disguise
until the day it returns to dust
when the charade is finally over,
the hard work done
after containing
such a fragile composition intact
for so long.

Maybe decaying is a sigh of relief
and death the curtain speech
before discovering
if after all these years,
the God I have learned to love
is more real
than I have ever been.

you are what you eat

The woman becomes girl again,

    becomes hungry again,

    becomes sapphire in the sanctuary again,

    becomes baptized again,

    becomes antagonized wind again,

    becomes unbecomingly,

and it's stupendous.

SHEEP IN THE MIDST OF WOLVES

savage wolves will come in among you,
and there will be
snatching and scattering,
weeping and gnashing of teeth

Confraternity's Resuscitation

I take the priest's homily mouth-to-mouth.
Redemption at the rate of resuscitation.

Brow submerged. Clammy beneath the expectations of two
   generations.
Forehead christened and baptized into a name I am later asked
   to lose.

Open wide. Throat all vacancy and no volition.
I make room for Father's hands,
offering tongue and testimony as appetizers
for the first of many mimicked Last Suppers.

Redemption doesn't cost much,
just ten spurts of *Hail Mary, full of grace*
and a pair of bruised knees during penance.
But that's only if I perch all pretty on the kneeler.

Make it to the finish line, and I'm in the club,
sealed into the shadow of a saint I selected with a dizzy finger.
Anastasia, the Deliverer of Potions.

It is only after I crawl across the catechism
I am told I will not be sent any Holy Orders.
No direct line to the Operator.

So I revoke my twisted knees and reclaim my first set of nine
   letters.
Empty my brow into the bin of borrowed dreams.
Start to bury myself in curiosity,
to cover myself with a question mark
and call it home.

genu(ine re)flection

In the building—the callous, the catalyst—known as church,
I first learned to *really* perform,
to give the audience a good show.

Right knee down, damp fingertips
tap, tap, tap, tap on my forehead,
sternum, left shoulder, right shoulder.

Saintly salutes in fear of the side-eye.
Yes ma'am, I haven't missed mass in three months.
I know you've been counting.

My charade of tranquility hidden behind
straightened blond hair and pink lace dresses.
We don't want Caucasian Jesus moaning in peaceful sacrifice
above the marble altar to be angry, now do we?

Heaven forbid I meet the King of the Jews
in his honest rage outside this stained-glass cage
and join this Man of Bread for some heavy liberation
among those hearts uncalcified by catechismal climbing.

the easter bunny and Jesus

must have a strained relationship.

Dangling together by a hare, two sneaks
stealing out from their burrows at break of day.

Pastel eggs casting shadows on the Passover.
Who is this cartoon coney hogging the spotlight?
Who called this kosher?

Osterhase, Eostre, and the King of the Jews
piled into vacant chocolate cottontails.
Shalom shuffled into staggered, ambiguous love songs.
Have a blessed holy day, a restful holiday,
as long as
you keep your religion   over   there.

In the name of the St. Valentine, St. Patrick,
and the not-so shriving spirit of Mardi Gras,
We wish you a Merry Santaclausmas!

Habits dye hard.
Hope dies softly, with a fleeting whisper,
or in the case of the Carpenter,
momentarily.

purgatory

You said you're familiar with dying
like you've done it before,
like resurrection was something
you could relapse into.

jump

Jack be nimble
Jack be quick
Jack just hurry and be done with it.

Zip up your pants,
your palms.
Don't you dare
arrive at penance panting like
the dog you are

Body of stainless steel. Spontaneously discharging.
Wielding violence because you had no choice but to yield.
You are the indulgence of a Father who cannot gird his loins.

The alb cascading into albeit.

Bearing the consequence of silent sufferings.
You have gone into labor
and will not be returning
anytime soon.

Memory, the unpurgeable purgatory.

You are the saber denying softness,
blackening into gunpowder like a Tennessee storm cloud.
    Bullets haunting sky.
    Screams like a muffled thunder clap.

You are called the problem, but I know the truth,
how you shot across the stratosphere
but couldn't make it over the candlestick,
failed to avoid the burn, so you
became the flame because
you couldn't run away.

When the holy fire
was forced down your throat,
you swallowed
and gulped
and gasped
because doesn't breathing fire
still mean you
made it out alive?

the burning man

The man burns and is blessed.
On fire for God. Doused in thoughts and prayers like gasoline.
Drinking from the hydrant of holy instruction.

We are emaciated enamel gawking at the enigma.

Bones sing about being at home with the Lord.
      Tell me, does home smell like cartridges kissing crayons?
      Does the doorbell sound like steel crunching bone?

The burning man does not smile.
The bells. Can you hear
the consecration bells?

Abednego.
He steps into the raging flames
faithfully chasing silence.
A cult classic.

the witches brew

Witches don't exist, but I know they meet
every second Monday down past Socrates Park.

The Italian bakery on the corner of Crescent Street closes at
   7:00 pm,
but the copper tabby cat cooing
under the belly of a potted peony just trying to survive
has told me about their secret sessions.

Sometimes, if you walk slow enough,
you can hear the crones chanting.

Peek through the doorjamb
to see arms raised, lost sheep bleating about
wanting to be on fire.

But who wants to join the aching of ash?
Who likes to reach the extension of two arms outstretched
only to find there is nowhere else to go?

Nowhere else to run.
No one else to be.

The old bats are always smiling,
and if they aren't smiling, they are crying.
Can't quite choose what kind of babel they need that day.

Sometimes, if I wait outside the door long enough,
the sorceresses invite me inside. I expect to tread lightly across
   pins and needles,
for bones and blood to brandish the walls, but their hollow
does not haunt my dreams at night.

Upon inspection, there are only books.
Those books, all the same. Some sort of sacred manual
made by men yearning to be God.

God bless 'em, these witches who worship waiting.
Women waiting for a man to come back
from beyond the grave (again).

it's not about the nail

Jesus shotgunning the Father's cup.
Third time is the charm.

Who is this man, this memory that was not bulletproof?
If the nails came for him, then surely they can pin me in.

Find the hammer and watch
the world run
despite her blistered feet.

Be anywhere but there, drifting above your limbs,
clambering in the quicksand of your doubt.

Self-deception leads to acceptance.
Appearance. At the foot of the dying Nazarene
stood only women who could withstand
the cruelty,
the violence,
the reality of the skin
surrendering to skull.

A Messiah, pariah, priest.
The least of these.

Miracle worker and home wrecker.
You cannot touch his cloak and be the same.

Who is this man? And where can I find the courage
to put rim to running? Drinking in the thick,
red wine as it *glugs, glugs, glugs*
down my throat.

A foretaste of deliverance.

Purification in Queens

This borough is the grandmother of red,
founded on stolen blood and the fiery lipstick of call girls
who sold their skin to buy big-girl guns, these honey bees
eager to swarm the hands of the men
who stung them first.

Here, I have learned about the value of the Queen of Clubs,
how you can never consume enough laughter
even if you sleep
with your mouth wide open.

The humor won't find your cracked lips in the darkness,
but the hurt will
at full throttle,
scoffing at the audacity of apologies.

The suffering will come to purify you,
dip you in the crucible of pain.
Sifting you.
Straining you down
to the tea leaves
until you can finally face your fate,
ready to learn the consequences of the religion you ascribe to.

In that moment, you will
squeak out a prayer for deliverance,
take hold of the dregs,
      like medicine
      like a miracle,
      and swallow them in one gulp.

Ashes and Asics

We're late.
We're late.
We're late.

Mass began 17 minutes ago, and the priest religiously ends
a minute before noon. We've missed the greetings,
the Penitential Act, and half of the first reading.

Peace I give. My peace I give you—

Mother never minds slipping into the back pews during the
 credo recitation,
dribbling holy water across her temple before assimilating into
the *rise, sit, kneel*
of the congregation. Mother says it's about intentionality not
 punctuality.

I believe in one, holy catholic and apostolic church—

For 14 years, when patrons would pry apart their jaws to receive
 communion,
instead of glaring at the gangly tongues thrust into hopeful
 redemption,
I would look down to see what shoes they were wearing.
Pink kitten heels, small tan suede boots (must be a size 5?),
gray and blue New Balances, black strappy stilettos.

What did one wear to plead for forgiveness?

Moses took off his sandals by the burning bush,
but now one must approach the altar with style,
grace, and an attempt to save face.

*I look forward to the resurrection of the dead and the life of the world
 to come.*

have you ever

shaved one leg but not the other?
turned one cheek but not the other?
forgiven one parent but not the other?
worshiped one god but not the other?

four valuable lessons from a church-girl

If I didn't know any better,
I'd say let's set the story straight.

Let's call the split seas of society exactly what they are:

RED.
Blood-thirsty red.
Going-for-your-jugular-in-debate red.
Hand-slapping-the-other-cheek red.
Patellae-bruised-from-being-pushed-down-onto-the-kneeler red.
Bible-thumping-fist-pumping-trauma-dumping red.

If I didn't know any better,
I'd say let me teach you something about holiness.

If I didn't know any better,
I'd expect you to listen.

There are four valuable lessons this church-girl can tell you.

ONE.	Obedience is an optical illusion.
	Therein lies the contradiction.
	To comply with a command, to submit to an authority,
	one must understand the direction and the director.
	Mere observance of the suggested action
	does not guarantee comprehension nor compliance.
TWO.	When prompted to sing gospel hymns,
	sing loud enough to hear your own voice strum.
	Then ask yourself, is it believable? Is it genuine?
THREE.	Be a woman with wartime kindness.
	There is a time to kill and a time to heal.
FOUR.	Be wary of chasing righteousness out of convenience.
	A sacrifice given out of excess is no sacrifice at all.

pennies from heaven

Flying like a bat outta hell,
outta the black lacquer combustion
barreling up my throat.

If prayer was a lover, we'd end up celibate.

Flashing sirens, whiplash from the backfire of a pistol
discharging after shooting stars.

Catch a penny soaring upward
out of the wishing well.
Slip it in your pocket and save it for a sunny day,
for a happier ending,
a once-upon-a-time that becomes
twice, three-times
reliable.

Echolocation.

Can you hear the whelp wailing behind the yellow wallpaper?
Nails like surfboards cutting into the waves,
clawing, scratching, searching
for an escape hatch.

popcorn prayer circles: a tragedy

PRAISE REPORT!

Amelia has agreed to go to church with me.
The ladies in the circle of cross-legged bodies bow their heads in vigorous excitement.

They say she is going to meet Jesus, but I'm still wondering
how mortals and mortar can summon this God of the Universe?
Has this prophet-gone-shepherd agreed to take flesh again?
Has Jesus started sending voice memos, because if so,
I still haven't heard from him
and mine is long overdue.

The ladies are splayed across a Pottery Barn carpet more valuable than my week's wages.
They ask me if Amelia has a spirit of heaviness.
I translate: *Is she depressed?*

I say, "I think so," but I know it's so much more than that.

It's eight years of depression, the agony which the word itself barely puts a dent into.
It's six years of deception from a lover that is not cunning but conniving.
It's 11 years of illness, infection, self-hate, and suicide ideation.
It's seven months of fucking with no feeling.
It's one week from hell.
It's loneliness.
It's a loss of purpose.
It's the damn medication.
It's the silent phone .... *why won't it ring?*
It's the late nights and the hazy bedroom.
It's her dinner being resuscitated across the threshold of her lips every night.
It's the internet telling her she is just like everyone else.

Reminding her how everyone else is in pain too,
but we all just play pretend.
So why can't you?

Why can't you?

SHE CAN LAUGH AT THE DAYS TO COME

charm is deceptive and beauty is fleeting
    charm is currency and beauty is notoriety
charm is deceptive and beauty is fleeting
    charm is currency and beauty is notoriety

my femininity is that kind of girl

My femininity was born and raised
under the arches at 46th and Bliss Street.

Two cheeks Sunnyside up.
She is the last sip of your IPA
leaving your mouth full of regret—or victory.
It depends if you consider backwash a blessing,
something to remind you where you came from.

Get on her bad side, and she will
make you bleed out of all the wrong crannies.
No lucky number seven train to shuttle you away.
No, not this time.

She will string you up by your hind legs in the parking garage
and start asking you questions like it's not your first time
at the rodeo, like it's not your first night in a jail cell.

My femininity is selectively domestic.
She does not cook.
She does not clean.
She does not work for free except when she pleases
or when she wants to be *that* kind of girl,
that kind girl,
that church-girl,
that nice-smile-on-the-sidewalk-how's-your-day-going girl.

That girl whose purse is a graveyard of Joe & the Juice receipts.
That girl who can estimate the latest M60 Select Bus she can take
without missing her flight.

But sometimes, she is less Barbie and more Bowser,
less Baby and more Billie.

Sometimes she is the girl who bites her nails and still paints them
  anyway,

who can give you a decent stick-and-poke
under the roaring purple light of her bedroom lava lamp.
My femininity enjoys being the girl who calls her grandma every
 single Tuesday
and still puts the DJ in reverse on the weekends.
Nowadays, she is not afraid to be her own best friend,
to be both go-go dancer and prayer warrior.

My femininity is like choking on a backhand at Arthur Ashe
 Stadium,
like running the lawnmower over your journal just to stock up
 on paper cuts.

She is no lemonade-sipping Sally.
She is a twice-used blue-Solo cup full of Sprite yelling
 "GOTCHA!"
She is both the hands holding your hair back as you dry-heave
and the reason you got so lovesick in the first place.

She is a boss-babe, bad-bitch,
main-character captain deep in her villain era.

She is irresistible and independent,
as delicate as glitter and tough as glass.

Touch her, and she'll make your ancestors dizzy.
Make you spin, twist, bop it, leaving you praying to meet your
 Maker.

Her body is not what it used to be, it's better,
but better does not fit into boxes nicely,
Better isn't always proud of living another day, older.
Better becomes strands of hair plastered into a blond cyclone on
 the shower wall

that girl who calls her mom because she is lonely in this big,
   rotting apple,
that girl who just wants someone to hold her hand
as she bleeds,
and bends,
and bows
but does not break.

little bean

Little bean burrowing down.
Dirty demon rearing its crunchy hair.
Did you find yourself a home?
Does it smell like you always pictured it?
Like vanilla bean candles on the stovetop,
seduction left to simmer,
passivity boiling over.

Little bean, does it taste nice?
Not his lips but yours
as they crack and falter
under the weight of the ordinary?

Little bean, you are already a mother.
Familiar with beginnings.
Already good at pretending to forget
how death will not fail to remember you.

Little bean,
little love.
Reaping where you do not sow.
Harvesting what you did not plant.

You have found yourself a home.
Dirty.
Damp.
Daunting but delightful.

bless your heart, do your part

The tokophobic has seven fallopian tubes in her uterus.

In the first, thousands of paper cuts from Mayo Clinic printouts.
The second is scorched with the ashes of burning men.
The trespass is not like the gift.

The third flume expands narrowly for the possibility of happiness by self-sacrifice.

The fourth is a trash chute
with a broken grandmother clock
that won't stop ticking.
Tocking.
Boom.

The fifth peels open at low tide. Shame kept at bay.
The sixth is chalk full of fantasies, vain daydreams, and seamless sleeps.
The seventh bulges with temporal interpretations of success.

How many years will it take to detach the virus from the host?
The fear of falling from the fruit?

a woman's place

In Queens, the mitéra tells the violins to stop playing.
She is the fist of God wrapped in a banner of silk.

She knows there are only two types of trash on the curb:
one that is worthless and the second
worthless to some but priceless to others.

The N line
        gradually
                rocks her to sleep.

This is how the borough that loves the number thirty says, "I
    missed you."

On Sundays, she hands out borrowed stars
to the bundled paidiá scampering down the street.

Her nurturing hands are always busy,
hair a coffee tumbleweed matted and tied back
with that orange and purple checkered headscarf.

She is the cistern and the celestial.
Heaven's unlikely spy maintaining, *my peace I give to you*
as if she was Mother Teresa back again,
resurrected to confront
this killing floor of concrete
we call home.

Her lungs live in contraction.
Battling the sirens of Mt. Sinai, she calls her children home
out from the grasp of Astoria's summer heat.

It must get lonely—holding the weight of that purple tongue
that makes any bodega cashier recoil in force.

She is the pawn promoted by guile.
The female sovereign, unobstructed and undeniable.

Loneliness, to her, is an acceptable risk.
Not all men can buck up to bear the weight of God's work,
to wrap the wounded fist in fine silk
even as it weeps,
to quiet the orchestra
when silence is the last thing
she would ever want to hear from God.

* *mitéra* [Greek], mother
** *paidiá* [Greek], children

Rosie, just Rosie

a woman's work
is just *work*.

She knows she will never
get the job done

when living
isn't a task that one
simply finishes

even if she
is dead tired
of trying.

the gloaming

Little Suz bends so far backward over the sun
the onlookers call it a sun assault.

Vertebrae tumbling at the speed of light.
She moves fast, fast enough to find the moon at midday.

Pour out the wine.
Let's drink to dancing.
Let's drink to golden slippers tipping down the throat.
Let's drink to the faded glory of sweet nothings,
to the portrait of a lady escaping the way of all flesh,
to the footsteps in the sand I took alone.

I ate the lip gloss because my mother
wanted me to be beautiful.

I hate how it tasted so good.
Strawberry kiwi,
tart and tangy,
the tease of affection.

All wink and no whisper.

An Ode to my Cervix

O Great Tongue of Femininity.
Guardian of Virginity.

You long-necked and thick-lipped lover who says *none shall pass*.
Yet, even in your off season,
birth tongues of fire.

Light a match, and watch the whole world
march into January under the banner of your ancestry.

Light a candle, and see winter
finally arrive in unreciprocated silence.

You are both seal and seduction.
Sensuality in a bodycon rose dress.
Feline fears clawing their way into the forefront of my identity.

Nine lives I never wanted,
at least not yet.

This one life
grand enough.

The All-American Girl is 28 days old

The Maxi pad and the Band-Aid are not friends.
They do not share an affinity
for allowing their sultry, viscous lips
to crimp one's skin and coddle the blood
bubbling out from my body.

Maranda teases me as we paint white birdhouses in Biology.
She caps the summit of my structure with a crimson bullet hole.
I feel the gunshot blow through a belly
which I have not yet learned to hate.

I close my eyes. The wound doesn't disappear.
Stabbed in the back by adolescence, I declare war against my body.
The combat continues to this day.

Armed with only the knowledge
provided by American Girl's *The Care and Keeping of You*,
I waddle into my mother's office.

She quietly slips me a teal, translucent package between my shaking hands.
Like a drug deal with no instruction manual, I stagger into the locker room
before 4th period gym to move from defense to offense
during this onslaught of womanhood.

At home, I tell my sister about
the four chaotic hours I've spent being a woman so far.
I ask her why so many people wear pads if they are so inadequate at sealing the leak?

She collects my hands in hers as we sit on the chilled, beige tile floor.
Her eyes loud with falling tears as she launches her incredulity:

YOU PUT THE STICKY-SIDE UP?

*private school p*ssy*

What doesn't kill you brings you to your knees,
brushes against the thigh-gap
you don't have.

Catch a falling star and let it burn in your pocket.
Feel it fade into warmth,
into memory,
leaving your skin
even colder than before
divinity pinched you.

Pierced.
No seam but all suture.
Camel galloping through the eye of a needle.
I am hanging on by a thread.

Knees sheathed in a silk skirt.
Fists full of safety pins
so I am not a risk
to the male gaze, I mean graze.

Why does appreciating my body make me a whore?
Hate the sin but love the sinner.
Hate the skin but love the thinner.

Is infertility infectious? Because I cannot conceive
nor accept this version of stripped normality.

The topic of modesty all hot and heavy in Christian conversation.
Decency wielded like a weapon.

I will not fall victim.
I will not destroy this temple. I cannot rebuild it in three days.
It would take me more than a lifetime.

My limbs are a growling beauty, the build of a loose braid draped over a sandy brick wall, a door happily succumbing to the weight of its hinges.

imago d(e)issent

I am a refugee within my ribs,
singing songs from a homeland
I have never left.

stačíš, zostaň moja zlatá

My gaze fogs the mirror, passes
through me like wind,
like coughing water,
my spitting image,
as I tenderly
keep on decaying.

*stačíš, zostaň moja zlatá [Czech],
 you are enough—stay my darling

*parked in the driveway of a house
    where I do not live*

I devour the nails and collect the timber.
Crucifixion by digestion.

It's raining—again, so I reassemble
my skeleton and build a forest.

The leaves scuttle to their canopies.
The bricks in my stomach retreat back into clay.
My eyes flutter open. The beckoning breeze
makes the poem written
out of despair
disappear.

This is how I bring the peace to my body
I have always wanted, by assimilation.

slits and ladders

Bad bunny.
Play boy, no consequences.
Play girl, but don't forget
to play
by the rules, girl.

Live by the ruler,
by the book
mark
set
spike.

Tag
you're it.

You've got *it*.
You made it.

Does it feel nice?
Is it everything you've ever wanted?
How is it going, being anything and everything people want you
    to be?

Are those happy tears?
Save them for a rainy day when no one will even notice
you're crying
        or they might, but at least
they won't bother you with the trouble
to ask if you're okay.

Thank God they have the decency to let you suffer alone,
too afraid that you might actually admit
how you carry a body racked by
abandonment
that wails and wails
until you become noise itself.

you can have it all (but not everything)

If the world is your oyster, pat that pearl and take a seat.
Let that briny tongue lick the plate empty
and damn it, take a breath.
Bake your cookie cake and eat it too.

You are not that cool-salad-gal, the one at the bar
who orders a cocktail that isn't even on the menu.

You are not the late-night-rave-raging-gal who doesn't mind
missing meals, doesn't mind staying up past 2:00 am
in a loud club where no one knows your name
or how many drinks you've had
or cares if you make it home alive.

You only live once
upon a time.

Take a picture. It'll last longer,
maybe long enough to pretend that life is worth living
                                        as you archive
                       and delete
           and backspace yourself
into near-oblivion.

The hallucination of a waning crescent smile
on the horizon of your name.

Bushwhacked and bedazzled,
you are praying to the saints of Progress.
Rest assured they want nothing else but for you
to maintain that empty blue bruise of belief,
trusting for a moment
that you can
have it all
but not everything.

HONOR YOUR FATHER AND MOTHER

do not provoke your children to anger
do not provoke your children, lest they get discouraged

Mother, may I?

Momma stands a stone's throw across the yard.
Sister and I are lined up by the mailbox
ready to brawl over who is the better listener,
who is the favorite,
who is going to blast off with Momma's blessing.

Sister is worried I will play like Jacob, stealing her firstborn rights
by the thin, blond whispers on my arms,
by the skin of my teeth.
The slack-jaw who has nothing to lose.

Mother, I call.
May I take two baby steps forward?
Mother, may I hop on my right leg three times?

No, she says. But I still have questions.
No, she says. But I ask them all the same.

Mother, may I ride to prom with the boy who smells like alcohol anyway?
Mother, may I ask my friends about the specifics of sex because you never speak about it?
Mother, may I know how the spark got kindled behind your eyes?
Mother, may I plug my ears as the TV roars in this house and it not be considered rude?
Mother, may I ask why you and Dad don't sleep in the same bed anymore?
Mother, may I go?
Mother, may I go, but I promise I'm going to come back.
I'll come back for you one day,
but Mother, may I?

Mother, I've got to go.
Mother, don't say no.

Mother, wait —
Mother, stop
Motherfucker, what has he done to you again?
What have you done to me?

I learned to pack my bags when I was eight.
The only difference now is that I have a few more kilos to carry,
a few more bags and a lot less time
to take them where I'm headed.

Mother, may I tell you about the places I'm going, or will you be heartbroken?
Mother, will you be happy for me?
Mother, will you mean it?
Mother, will you smile with your canines but leave your eyes limp and lonely?

Mother, do you still believe in fairy tales?
Mother, do not go all Pinocchio on me and tell me you're fine.
Mother, I am a real girl, but obedience is both a virtue and a villain.
Mother, do you see the yellow brick road I took out of this Valley of Ashes?
It may not have taken me to the Promised Land,
but I found the Promise Maker.

Mother, may I stay over here just a little bit longer?
Mother, there is so much to tell you about this place.
This world, it isn't fair, but it's far better than I thought it'd be.
Mother, there is so much space here to fail.
Mother, it's terrifying and it's wonderful.

Mother, will you keep dying your hair black?
Mother, will you keep dying?

Mother, will you stay young forever?
Mother, will you stay forever in this city that was never yours to
    begin with?
Mother, may I ask why you stayed?

Mother, may I know what made you so afraid of your own body?
Is it the same disease that makes me terrified to touch my own?
Mother, what is it you are so scared of?
Mother, why can't you tell me?

Why can I not hold your pain the way you nurse and mend my own?
Why do you hide behind those brown tadpoles
swimming, swimming,
drowning
in all that foggy white light?

I have seen you vulnerable and unprotected,
stolen glances through bathroom door
as you slouch in despair in front of the vanity,
as you sit naked in a tub of lukewarm bath water
only up to the backs of your knees, afraid you'll use up all the hot
    water.
Afraid he will yell at you.
Afraid you might be the final straw.
I have seen how drained you are.
I have seen the way you look at him,
the way you speak to each other like it's mortal combat.
Sister and I caught in the crossfire.
Wildfires burning on both sides of the road.
Which one do we put out first?

Mother, are you burnt out?
Are you tired?
Mother, may I help?

May I hold some of that fatigue?
Mother, may I come home for a bit?
Mother, my receding Willow Lake.
Mother, will you listen to me this time and trust me?
Mother, will you admit that sometimes you don't know best?
Mother, don't you know that's okay?
Mother, don't you know how much I love you?
Mother, may I love you like that?
Mother, may I?

the hummingbird and the meadowlark

Tongue covered in brass tacks licking up the bullets.

Hole-punched, college-ruled.
I was a good student, meaning, I was destined
to work myself into extinction.
Caught in the crossfire.

Hand out compliments strung to fishing line
so when fear dawns,
you can reel them back
to stave off the loneliness.

If the girl screams in a laundry room,
but no one is around,
did she even suffocate?

Observe:

Pig-tailed princess slapped with the nickname bitch
sending smoke-signals from Sarah's backyard.
I spit out the word, this weapon against womanhood.
But the letters linger. They still splay themselves
within my ribs without languishing.

2002 gives us a sticky summer, so we play inside.
Sarah decides to teach me what it's like to kiss.
Hands-on research.
I'm introduced to intimacy with the scientific method.

Hypothesis:

If I can hide my teeth and puff out my chest like the stars on TV,
then I will not only get my crush (Dillon) to like me,
but I'll start to like
this type of physical affection too.

MATERIALS:

    A locked closet door
    A pink and white toy trunk
    A quilted blanket
    An empty brown house in the neighborhood cul-de-sac

CONTROL:

The girl writing this poem sits alone in bed afraid of the dark.

EXPERIMENT:

Three sweaty afternoons of youthful giggling.
Practice makes perfectionism.

They didn't tell us how kissing
is just whispering *I'm not going anywhere*
into someone else's wounds
and by anywhere, I mean
        into the arms of another lover,
and by lover, I mean
        empty shot glasses pulling soaked question marks down
        and starving them into exclamation points.
        Do you trust me? Do you trust me!

ANALYSIS:

Kissing is better when no teeth are involved.
Tongues are slimy and gross.
Brothers can be so annoying and nosy.
Friendship and kissing betray one another.

CONCLUSION:

My mother tells me Sarah's family still lives in that brown two-story nestled among the gossiping kudzu in the cul-de-sac.

I haven't seen Sarah since that same snug summer
when we sat in the back of her mom's car and decided
to stop playing like *that*, to quit locking doors
and hiding in pink toy chests.
Afraid to be called naughty, caught breaking suburbia
into more than just two pieces.

God forbid the children be curious,
to ask directly with their hungry mouths for answers.
Eager to know what love tastes like
when their parents seem so ravenous for it
but cannot seem to find it, can't swipe
the gift from the horse's mouth
out of fear of the bite.

one can of Canada Dry with a neon pink straw

I am fearless with a pair of scissors, ready to slaughter
anything from synthetic bags to expired credit cards.
The sea turtles will not die
trapped in the plastic collar of lucrative corporations
who really make you work for a bottle of pop.

My grandmother always called it pop, calls it pop.
She is still here with us, *thank God*.

Shirley remains as crafty as ever, stealing disposable spoons
in bulk from KFC. Complimentary gratuity
is what makes a meal taste so good.
She is ready at any moment
to sip, spoon,
slice, wipe, dab, or pierce
that which she finds her liking.

Shirley and I share
the same sense of style,
the same loathing of dark-washed skinny jeans,
the same resentment for absent fathers,
the same love of rollerblading at midnight
telling the boys
who ask us to dance
that we barely even know them
before we shimmy all night into rumors of dawn.

I'm petrified imagining the day
when she won't have her neon pink plastic straw
through which she will sip wind and wonder
down into her lungs (*God please let her breathe*)
and that I won't be there to fetch one
out of her pocketbook, that my scissors

won't be strong enough to cut
the translucent grip of death
to stop her
from choking
as she is dragged
out to sea.

she only grows near water

The sidewalk ends in the alleyway of my father's teeth.
Back turned like a magician
hiding throwing knives and turtle doves.

What did not kill me birthed into a warning label.

Unspoken fantasies
prematurely condemned
by the patriarchal tongue feeding me fire.

I catch the whiplash chilled on my cheek.
I take space.

I bend my other cheek into willowed submission.

Juvenile palms sealed to the sacrum in self-soothing.
Fingers failing to foil the geyser of a hot-spring rage.

I spout into the expanse between us 57 reasons
he cannot find me in the smog of his mirrors or memories.

Spilled sewage. Putrid smoke leaking from my nostrils.
I count the valleys I have hiked alone.
Pluck the hatred from my hands
until the concrete dries.

You'll never be able to do anything without me.
His words soggy on my chest.
Runes doused in black—wrapped in caution tape.
A gift of warning.
Folly in the costume of wisdom.

Watch me.

I spit into the heated blaze
and leave him to tend to the embers.

switchblade

On your wedding day,
it will be strenuous to remember
your almost-husband's face at the end of the aisle,
much harder than people
claim it to be.

Before the doors unlatch from their timber embrace,
your father grows tall next to you
in a black Navy uniform
despite the North Carolina heat.

He will apologize (twice)
for not being a better father.

You will spend your final minutes of singleness
consoling him,
forgiving him,
mourning the blade
you became in his absence.

Two tempers cut from the same cloth.

The wooden doors groan
and swing wide
to reveal
hundreds of plastered grins eager to light the sparklers
as you put away the duct tape
and run toward the man
you will now call home.

gone girl and what would've been her eulogy

inspired by Warsan Shire's "backwards"
and Sylvia Plath's "mad girl's love song"

The poem begins with the girl opening her eyes,
the world resuscitated—something created from nothing.
She is introduced to her reflection.

The girl of 28 walks her ballistic body
backward out of the bathroom.
This is what we call an answered prayer.

Silence.
BANG!
Scissors, paper, rock.

The depravity of mid-twenties depression
simmers into a tidepool of adolescent growing pains.

I can tell you how the glass is resurrected from the bloody sink.
Crystal chaos resuming its origin of nested vanity.
That empty, echoing slate
spits the girl back into beginnings.

Can you hear the dirge crawl back inside the mouth?
How else would you describe a burial gone birthday?

Corpse surfacing from soil to speak in rhymes once again.
Stiff body bleached with second chances.
Time studies the cadaver for regret.
Diagnosis: death by consumption.
In the lungs, a list of people
the girl devoured
during all her heedless living.

Open clavicles.
Bared canines.
The girl-gone-animal slithers
back into the shower baptismal and comes out striding.

Meanwhile, the paralytic man in Capernaum
sits down and never walks again.
Jesus of Nazareth exits the tomb,
carries the cedar cross back into Jerusalem,
and resumes his Passover feast.

The girl of 27 traces the ancestry of her tears back to Bethesda.
Youthful bones bouncing again with buoyancy.
No longer drowning,
She watches how the metropolis dims.
The city that doesn't sleep becomes a daydream.
Manhattan melting from a memory into a distant mirage.

> Telophase in the concrete jungle runs wild
> as the One World Trade Center
> splits into a pair of steel skyscrapers,
> for a brief moment, birthing planes
> to send commuters in pantsuits back home
> for a surprising Tuesday holiday in September.

The poem, no the parable, returns to the girl of 26
asking her husband if she is beautiful.
Five years pass.
The couple separates and never see each other again.
Name of the maiden regurgitating in the rear of her throat.
Patience lodged between wisdom teeth.

Meanwhile, the girl of 18 shrinks back
into the shroud of a punchline.
She writes herself a joke to make the pain more logical.

Like the whipping laughter of a hurricane is something she can
   control.
Like lightning could be a gentle lover.

The girl's father flies back from Germany,
takes off the Army uniform,
takes off the mask of cynicism,
takes off to Arizona for 17 months and comes back
to fall irrevocably in love with his wife.
He decides to stay forever.

The girl of 14 finally learns to love her own frame
with a forever kind of love.
Skin like stomata,
self-healing the scars
made from adolescent claws
when she became the blade.

She puts the blade down.
She picks it up.
She shaves her legs until eventually the bleeding stops.

Give the girl a mile,
and she'll only move an inch.

The priest saunters back into the cathedral.
Sweaty knees peel off the prie-dieu.
Consecrated bread whizzing back out from a hundred infected
   maws.
Holy water precipitates from the girl's furrowed brow.
Drips back into the golden bowl.
Her prayers become simple, strong, and sincere.

Cottontop head brightening like sunrise.
The girl of 11 moves back into the big white house on the hill
and dares to dream again.

She is 17 and trusts her dad not to break another TV / *even
though he will.*
She is 15 and believes Luke will take her out to the movies / *even
though he won't.*
She is 23,
and 19,
and 6.

She is desperate to cheat death,
to successfully hide from decay
among eight billion people / *even though she won't.*

The girl's name gets towed
back into the eddies of her mother's tongue.

The girl just barely-here
slinks back into her mother's womb
and signals it is safe for her sister
to follow her inside.

Darkness no longer a fear but a comfort.
The girl, no the idea of the girl,
gently loses her senses,
shrinks into perfect circumference,
no more pain, but extinction is not heaven.

Perhaps the opiate of oblivion
is not all it's cracked up to be.

coal for Christmas

It is December, but we are not celebrating Jesus' birthday.
Today, we put on our best clothes to make grief more appealing.

Ten bodies drifting in vicious silence before we head down
the road to All Saints Catholic Apostolic Church, before we
shake the hands of men who knew our PaPaw bathed in soot
and smiles as he worked in the old coal factory for a wage
that is illegal now, in a building that only exists in the town's
collective memory.

I watch my grandmother attempting to say goodbye
to this man she still loves
who is not breathing.

I am furious at God
for the death of a good thing.
Breathe, dammit.
PaPaw, you were always so good at it.

We sit in the church kitchenette telling stories I can no longer
remember
over tears sprouting a life of their own in the boiling aftermath
of grief.

The casket, left open.
White and polished, just like he wanted.

My dad reminds me how expensive funerals are,
asks me not to let him rot in the green meadows of the city I
was raised in.
Four months later, he calls and asks what I want from his will.
No, I do not want your horse, I just want you to stay.
Please, stay.

My mother cannot take her eyes off the body of the man who raised her. As we hold hands in the sanctuary, I wait for the bones to stop playing this cruel joke, for his toes to reappear after diabetes mercilessly stole them during Easter 2011. He always loved to walk, to push me down the hill on my purple bicycle and carry me back up the road to do it all over again.

Let's play PaPaw, I don't like this kind of game.

Mother lights a tall candle, one of the translucent pink fancy ones that costs $3 and has a real matchstick besides the kneeler. A prayer slithers out between her lips in a tongue heavy with anguish. I bow my head and do the same, learning this bend-by-bend procedure to extract suffering.

The sky bids us adieu. Cemetery dirt smeared against our black shoes.
For the first time in years, my mother doesn't tell me to freshen up.

It is evening and morning on the fifth day of this new normal. Mother, father, sister, cousins, aunt, grandmother, and uncle are all under one roof. A December miracle. The men are solemn, shaking hands. The ladies hug one another under the single-stringed lightbulb in this damp basement that is now just my grandmother's home.

Somehow, we are all laughing.
Cavernous creatures trying to stave off the sorrow with rancorous noise.
The kind of roar that might just
cause a resurrection.

midnight among the masses

Tardy and a bit tipsy.
It's already tomorrow, but here we are,
sliding into the pews wearing our pristine burgundy and black.

Yes Momma, my skirt is skimming my knees.
Hair curled like it is pageant day.
What trophy wife is going to win big tonight?

Wet foreheads and a chalice of wafers.
Dad hasn't crossed through this Red Sea since Palm Sunday 2006.

What do you mean I can't drink the blood but I can eat the flesh?
Jesus is strong, but Momma says germs are stronger.

Light a candle for Papaw.
Light a candle for Mary and her strong loins.
Light a candle because Momma said it's just what we do.

It's protocol.
It's parish participation.

It's the burning bush blown out,
the cold earth beneath my feet.

Sandals slipped back around my coarse heels.
The time for holy ground now a bygone
in the thunderclap of this
midnight rain.

La Cara Norte

Sweet little Anna.
She blinks all the time.
Hueco eyes gasping for air across the river.

The false indigos begin awakening in congregations on the shoreline
telling tales of the splendor that comes from flooding your soul in
   freedom dirt,
river clay the color of pastel de chocolate
as you swing, swing
swing, and then

j u m p.

The Rio Grande is bloated this time of year.
Bikes and bodies knocking up against the bank
in fives, tens, and twenties.
Steel and skin pushed down the emerald queue,
what those red-knuckled neighbors call that dandy line.

A country argues if this flower is a weed
worth being plucked or a daisy
meant to be protected.

Living is expensive and exhausting.
Little Anna marries this fatigue
into a family business
making Christmas in April a regularity.

The Jitterbug Jukebox Queen starts copy-pasting adobe homes
for the other women with hollow stares
who have made it to El Paso, Passageway to the North.

This clamoring city of promise and prejudice
charged with hundreds hoping to summit La Cara Norte,
and in doing so, be reborn into the
road less traveled.

surrogacy

the house is a hushed lullaby / I know every lyric / by hearth / seared into memory / do you remember in Pirates of the Caribbean when Jack showed on his arm where he was branded? / I bet even the sea is desperate for rain sometimes /

I was never the daughter who could stand still for a family portrait / say cheese / say gouda / tell me it's all going to be okay / buck up / you're fine / you fucked up, again / the sugar pavilion crashing down all around us / I guess even daylight comes when it's not wanted / all splinters and no tweezers / casual contamination /

bless your heart because it's been dying all this time / bless my heart because it's been crying all this time / I've been grieving you for decades / each time you've been resurrected, I wonder which one of you has come back to play / praise report / I am the golden calf made from the fire of your tribulations / I am the abyss and the absence / I am the surrogate of dreams I wish to abort / I am the shift key / delete, delete, delete / I am Martha too busy and too worried / I am the girl who does not know how to say no /

hush little baby / shush, don't say a word / mature into the mockingbird / keep evolving in rapid succession / speed up the song / life is what you make it / put some skin in the game / sleep when you're dead / papa's gonna buy you a cart and a bull / work hard or you're hardly working / have you made it yet? / you'll be the sweetest peach in town / don't you cry / don't forget to win big / don't you dare say a word / hush little baby, don't cry / don't cry / don't you fucking cry

a man of your word

Have you ever met a man more story than solid?
More simile than sinew?

My father is this man.
This metaphor.
This better-than-mediocre medicine keeping my heartbeat elevated
when the doctor says it's not supposed to hurt like that.

Loving shouldn't look like locked doors.
Loving shouldn't turn off the TV with a fist through the Cowboys
    on fourth down.
Loving shouldn't taste like my own tongue coddled in the eulogy of
    I-told-you-so.

Dad, you are a man of your word,
damned in the belly of a whale
you pretend does not exist.
And so, you shout
because it's the only way
you know how to say you're hurting.

All that bile.
All that burying.
Six feet isn't that deep after all.

Where are you putting the pain these days?
Buried in the blue stomach of a '54 Chevy?
Tucked and tipped hot down the back of your throat
during your Thursday morning coffees downtown?

You are roaring like an adjective refusing a noun,
pushing away the martini in favor of the olive.

But when the olive isn't pitted, what happens next?
Do you bite your tongue or curse and spit it out?

too many fathers

Why should I care to know this intangible, merciless, conjectured tyrant of the universe?

Why should I adopt another Papa when I already have far too many?

Perhaps because I do not have enough faith to be an atheist.

Perhaps the presence and the power reclining out there in the heavens is begging to be met.
Perhaps there is a strong case for a Creator.
Perhaps there was a man that lived no lies.
Perhaps the weight of glory cannot sit well on my shoulders without assistance.
Perhaps there was a Jewish, beautiful outlaw who is worth studying.
Perhaps the cost of discipleship is something I can pay.
Perhaps the *Screwtape Letters* analyzed the human condition correctly.
Perhaps we are all slouching toward Bethlehem.
Perhaps there are liturgies of hope that expose my deepest desires.

Perhaps *Mere Christianity* is worth exploring.
Perhaps having one more Father is worth considering.

SHE WHO HAS EARS, LET HER HEAR

many longed to see what you see, and did not see it
many longed to hear what you hear, and did not hear it

better, richer, fuller

How do I explain the aftertaste of swallowing the whole world
and still feeling hungry?

Let's call it the vacancy of a soul post-penance.
Let's call it a day in the life of my father.
Let's call it the dissatisfaction of sunrise.
Let's call it the American Dream.
WE DID IT BABY.

Dream on.
Pound those proud clenched fists into picket fences.

Dream until you realize
the dream was never yours
to wish to come true.

Soon the moment will arrive when you are surrounded
by white-washed partitions
dancing in cement.

How the neighbors will stare,
wondering who is this creature wailing
in the cage of grass clippings
that you hoped
would be greener
snipped and collected   from the other side.

the swan song turned to stone

There is sand buried in both brown Smartwool hiking socks
the cashier claimed would remain uncompromised
while roaming deep in the doorless woods.

So much sand.
All this time I can't get off me.

On this innocent morning in June,
I drink coffee and watch the ants, I mean people,
clamber up the stone bodyguards of Yosemite Valley.
This great severance that was never America's to begin with.

I watch those helmeted hopes
cling to these granite gifts of God
with such force you'd think
they'd die if they let go.

It's only five thousand feet.
There's a lot you can learn from that kind of congregation, I
    mean elevation.

Like how everyone prays in the end.

the hill he dies on

The boy does not yet know he is gentle
and how that is beautiful.

The girl checks the deadbolt
one, two, three times
and locks herself in the yellow duplex.

The boy is told to become a man,
but that is what he is afraid of most.

Men, passive and power hungry.

The boy instead becomes the house on the hill,
lights himself on fire to help others find their way back home,
      even if home is a pile of ashes,
      even if home is a pilfered orange bottle
      beckoning in twilight ahead of schedule.

A car full of teenagers rolls down dark Halloween streets.
Blood streams all treat
until the trick appears.
It's not so funny to watch
skeletons exploding from skin.

The girl confronts the finality of death.
Maybe life is not that sweet,
or perhaps even bones get lonely sometimes.

The boy and the girl befriend winter,
harboring cold shoulders just to make it out alive.
      Blistered shoulders bent toward Zion.
      Shoulders yoked with holy words soggy with unbelief.
      Where is this God, this consuming fire who sees?

The boy and the girl stand blood-soaked
and compromised
and confused.
The sanguinary exchange becomes a sanctuary.

The boy begins to believe he is tender and strong.
The girl dares to leave the locks undone. The bolts bygone.

Even if death is imminent.
Even if goodbyes and badbyes coexist
because drowning
and deliverance
are two tides of the same sea.

casual morbidity

I wail for the brutality of missed goodbyes,

the
                                        tragedy

       of

               staggered

                         living.

All this decaying—

I covet your laughter
and ache for soft evenings.

Everything is temporary and fickle.

Will we awaken from the lie of permanence
when the body bleeds black
and the ink flows red?

is this what they call depression?

When I used to drive over the I-5 bridge,
      I would sometimes imagine

what would happen if I drove
      over the concrete ledge

and like a bullet,
      burrowed myself into the depths

where water greets flesh
      just to see who would apologize first.

salvation through repetition

FAITH as in, the epilogue of sun.
FAITH as in, the resolution of my mother's shoulders to be a
    wife only once.
FAITH as in, my hell-bound hunger for hedonism heaving me
    away from heaven.
FAITH as in, my grandmother mailing me Crest toothpaste,
    Tic Tacs, and Kleenex for my birthday.
FAITH as in, the books and people I love bending backward
    and lighting their own pages aflame.
FAITH as in, the addictive splintering of mirrors.
FAITH as in, the regularity of All Saints Church Lenten Fish
    Fry Bingo Marathon.
FAITH as in, my sister's pleasure for holding hands.
FAITH as in, my father meeting God underneath the abdomen
    of his yellow 1950s Cadillac.
FAITH as in, my heart hurling toward the sun

        like a spider with web in tow.
        Translucent and temperamental tendrils
        whipping wind like David charging Goliath,
        carrying the bold assurance that I will
        make the light my own.

squall—a localized storm, a loud cry

Deflowered, lost bloom
of innocence given away.
Both bud and stem.

Entire root systems upheaved
in the name of love.

Knees making
tracks in the snow.

I am numb and the world
caught in the amorphous
white sameness.

the day the moon fell

The day the moon fell, I was asking for an amen.
A holy so be it.

Horse shit.
I was busy drowning in the bay of a question mark
roaming the shadows of Socrates Sculpture Park with a dry mouth,
pleading with God,
whispering words
the weight of lingerie,
begging to be loved like lace,
      softly
      tenderly
      graciously.

The day the moon fell,
there was no heartbeat in that lipstick eclipse.
Stillborn lullaby collapsing out of that little black
celestial dress doused in silver confetti.

The sea tides left in havoc,
not knowing what to do
with this unrepressed freedom,
no longer told
      how
      or when
      or where to be stirred.

The day the moon fell, I jumped off the swingset in Astoria Park
and landed somewhere off the coast of Lima,
close enough to see the city of lights
shimmering without apology,
bubbling with a language
I hold a close acquaintance.

The day the moon fell, I was thinking about death—again.
How all good things
must not only come to an end
but come to the end of themselves for their own righteousness.

True goodness must be a hot commodity
to maintain its reputation.

The day the moon fell, I was in Queens and became one.
Reserved. Projecting false confidence.
Pretending to memorize and utilize the word "stop" as I pleased.
I pinched my cheeks to make it seem like "no" was a good time,
like I am the girl who wears blush just for the fun of it,
like giggling isn't so hard these days,
like there is no iPhone note with dates and people that make me
   weep,
like I am the cherry tree
and not the black horse,
not the animal
trapped in the middle of nowhere
asking strangers to love me
after all these years
even as they cry:

No, no, no, no, no, no.
No, no, you're not the one for me.

speed dial

Porcelain palms in protest.
The ceramic crusade to fight off sleep with vinegar.
A sour taste for rest.

Fear I will soil the bed into a coffin
full of confessionals.

Tell me, is there a direct line to Providence?

Dial tones humming me lullabies
birthed from the lips of my mother
now stanzas
laboring in me,
bloating my body into forests.

Somewhere, a tree falls,
and everyone observes its collapse with pity.

I mourn by the roots.
Take a branch as a memento.
A souvenir.

A reminder of our common unearthing
and the uproar of our collective downfall.

BLESSED ARE THOSE WHO MOURN

for they will grieve
and grieve
and grieve,
but they will be comforted

slipstream

In the emergence of summer,
I rinsed love with obsession until it drowned.

I scrubbed the hours and counted my hands
until denial graced me with her presence.

Fingers flattering the Grand Canyon
with their microscale replica upon my digits,
designating me Mother Earth, as if I could do more
than staple eggshells back together
and live as one
seemingly unbroken.

Not the hammer threading nails into the haft.
Not the pillowcase smothering the sheets.

I took a census of our apartment
and found your leavings everywhere:

>   in the naked oak drawers,
>   in the spare silver keys shrieking on the table,
>   in the pregnant silence.

But before you left to begin again,
you rearranged resentment.
Placed it on the coffee table as if I wouldn't see
the pile of clenched fists.

You buried extra footsteps in the burgundy rug
as if I was not familiar with the route of abandonment,
as if I needed a cemetery of you.

pulp fiction

Orange like the city, no like the county,
like the matching tattoos we have nested into our creases.

Pulp fiction. Pith stashed between the cracks.

Orange like tabby cat chasing mouse and winning.
Orange like a question.
Orange like daylight bursting forth
through a translucent locust wing and crooning anyway.

Citrus kissing in the backyard on two moving limbs.
Swinging, dangling cautiously.
Danger, lightly salted.

Orange like your grandmother's blush.
Orange like the velvet seat of the antique church organ in the
  Winston Chapel downtown.
Orange like the wool scarf I never wore to that Clemson
  football game but kept in my dresser.

Orange. Not quite lustful like burgundy
nor holding the simmering curiosity of yellow.

Orange like spring's tulips or fall's squash.
The birth and death of seasons,
blood caught red-handed
rushing against the peel to hold the line.

Orange, second-best.
Always second.

Orange like the tiger in me ready to tear apart the monarch I'm
  protecting.
Orange like a secret you cannot keep for more than a week.

Cunning orange, burnt but still claiming the name Beauty.
The color of greeting and grieving.
Entering and exiting.

Orange like the city, no like the county,
like the matching tattoos we hold in our creases
and squeeze tight, tight, tight.

drunk on rejection

One cup of hibiscus tea
      between two hands for
           three minutes past four.

    It has been five weeks
trying to make this town home.

In six hours, I will
      fall asleep again
           only to rise at seven
      to make another cup of hibiscus tea
before eight hours of work
      during which I will do my best
           to remember
    the nine reasons
I moved to this city
      and how they outweigh
           the ten lies
    I have mistakenly believed
about myself today.

a life worth dying for

I love this park where I can eat strawberries in the silence of a screaming city. Where pizza and wedding planners congregate to make moments happen. Memories, something happy to place in frames on fireplaces that don't exist in this town. This place where glass reflections merely add to the illusion of the grandeur of getting all we've never wanted and nothing we've ever needed.

If the grass could speak, what would it say of our discontentment? Would the baristas accuse us of all the bruises we've harbored from this restless town? This island of empty promises takes your granite and makes gravel. It'll leave you groveling for the return (not of Mercury) but of simplicity, for an affordable price for tennis shoes, for the smell of something besides urine, for faces that actually stare back at you long enough to see you.

Sometimes, in this city made of steel resolution and insatiable appetites, I realize I am not lonely enough in all the right ways and desperately solitary in all the wrong ones.

new age apocrypha

At 4:00 am, the city's decrescendo
tumbles through my bedroom window.
The night gently returns to coals.

If you listen closely, you'll hear
the muffled blaze spit psalms
from the embers of the day.

The hymns left out of the holy
scriptures. The laments of unbearable
loneliness written in a room
full of smiling socialites

> in a city where strangers easily lose
> > the end of themselves in the beginnings of
> > others.

> in a world more bound to everyone else than
> > we had originally bargained for.

I listen to the soft groans of this city I call home.
Sacred spillage settling into silence
leaving me alone at first light.

nights like these

The night ripens with anticipation.
Nights like these, the grass is greener where it rains.
Nights like days, when people love you
quietly, with cheese pizza
at boozy book clubs
in a city that doesn't care
whether or not
you are
here

                          or if you are alive

                to feel the numbing glory of nights like these
when I have never felt more awake.

how are you?

Like lavender,
susceptible to a hundred little violences.
A handful of bloomings.

Dozens of winnowings later,
once softened by moonlit walks at midnight,
a deep lilac sprouts from my elbows.

Mulberry and sangria flood my clavicles
clothing me in amethyst.

Never quite royalty
but not without dignity.

food poisoning

Fork sauntering past my cheeks.
Rappelling down my throat.

Curiosity uncoiling
until it breaches
my stomach
to
see
if
the
exodus
within
me
is
dissolving
on schedule.

clothespin

You smell like California Poppies.
Like a miracle waiting for a mother.
Like a prayer waiting for an answer.

Icarus

I am the alpha, which is to say,
the beginning of a new word yet undefined.

The rhythm of three birds fluttering to the sky
fighting for the fame of Icarus.
The first kiss of daybreak.

It tastes like hope, like a wave
that has never licked dry sand,
which is to say:

Undefeated.
Roaring.

incandescent autumn

The mountains have gone copper.
The leaves bitter ginger burned by time once again.
Indeed, the whole earth approaches a genesis.

THE VALLEY OF THE SHADOW OF DEATH

The voice cries out in the wilderness.
"Son of man, can these bones live?"

And behold, a rattling.

a list of things that haven't managed to kill me (yet)

- my unrequited crush on Diego in 11th grade
- sleeping in my Jeep Cherokee at California reststops
- crying while driving home in a torrential deluge of hail
- razor blades
- the I-5 bridge haunting the skies of Portland, Oregon
- getting trapped inside an RV closet for three hours at Camping World
- ocean riptides
- choking on Cape Cod salt & vinegar chips
- the sixth pitch of Exum Ridge on the Grand Teton
- loneliness (because marriage doesn't mean you aren't lonely)
- the fear of being unliked
- FOMO
- toxic shock syndrome
- the anonymous Miss North Carolina voy forum
- the cougar I met while hiking Mount Adams
- snow blindness
- adult-size vitamins
- falling in love
- falling out of love
- the lies I too easily believe about myself
- tthe bathroom scale I used to have (but think about often)
- the weight of my NYC commuter backpack
- airlines and their metal sky tubes I do not trust
- being followed home at night
- being followed home during the day
- my self-deprecating guilt for never doing enough
- whitewater kayaking skirts
- audition rejection
- skiing on slopes far above my ability level

- an unalterable love for Nestle cookie dough
- the embarrassment of publicly bleeding through my pants
- dental office checkups on my fillings
- the hollowness of social media
- the weight of being underappreciated

the realities of death: an exhaustive list

I think of the saddest story I could write, and I think of you.

There are no stages of grief, only cavities of loss scabbed and scorched. Wine stains on a white table cloth. Tip you over and watch you pour out. Flip it over and pretend everything is as it was.

Banksy once said you die twice, but I think we kick the bucket three times.
  #1 The sky exiting your lungs and not returning.
  #2 Your name falling off someone's tongue for the final time.
  #3 Deciding not just to endure death but find freedom in it.

Steel spooning glass on the 78th floor. Being late to work can be a blessing.

Addiction is the gateway to immobility on the path of pleasure.

No, he is not coming back. Yes, you could've answered the phone, but you didn't. And if it happened all over again, you still wouldn't have picked up the line.

Death is the descendant of thieves, the child of divorced loves. It has been stealing from you since your first breath, and ever since, sits curled like a troll under the bridge waiting for you to pass by.

Skeletons will never lie to you. It's people that will.

Point Nemo is the furthest place from any living being. Its coordinates are 48°52.6'S and 123°23.6'W. It serves as an underwater graveyard for falling space debris and for mistakes our civilization wishes to forget.

The only assurance in life is that we shall all find stillness in the end.

supposed thoughtcrimes that leave Winston gagging in his sleep

Someone will die when it's inconvenient for you. You will get mad about it. Then you will realize the person you love is dead. You will realize how death is the larger inconvenience.

Your medicine is not helping you. It is giving you an alternate
way to die.
Your medicine is not healing you. It is giving you the pestilence of addiction.

Traveling is either exceedingly restful or a channel overrated escapism draining one's finances.

There will be someone you loved that never loved you back. You will never stop asking yourself (even after marriage and kids and cities sheltered in for decades) what would've happened if that one person would have reciprocated that affection way back when.

a lie is   a lie is   a lie is   a lie is   a lie is   a lie is alive

Sunsets are the surest reminder how even the brightest light cannot escape death. We marvel at its finality with a subconscious sense of empathy.

Sex is too hyped up by culture.
It is not the best way to keep your relationship alive, interesting, and intimate.

The tale of Hansel and Gretel is a story of child abandonment and cannibalism.

We say "I love you" as the door closes, as the phone lines click, as the Jeep putters down the street, as the bedroom light sizzles out, as the dancers hit their marks, as the plane engines accelerate, as the head stacked with ponytails skips down the school hallway because we are aware that finales do not announce themselves but, instead, take your breath away when you least expect it.

despite all things, a profession of faith

inspired by Abigail Carrol's "Creed"

I believe in the importance of dawn,
the captivating silence of elevator rides,
and the death of art by applause.

I believe in the mighty generosity of God,
in snotty prayers at 2:00 am and long airport goodbyes.
I believe in the weight of an unread book in your palm,
in the potency of truth
and the power of forgiveness.

I believe in second chances and endless changes,
in divine resurrection, in the marvel of scribbled words
and highlighted pages.

I believe in the elegance of selfless love,
the accountability of Post-it notes,
and the laughter of late-night Polaroids.

I believe in the mothering hush of museums,
the time machine of a lover's name,
and the worship of a God who gives grace to the rebellious,
who cares for his afflicted creation with affection.

I believe in hope—despite all things.

I believe in hope and that this belief isn't naive or in vain
but, instead, the nativity of a full and purposeful life.

the last, unforgettable line of a nonexistent story

It was then she met God and realized her labor and languishing were not in vain.

NOTES

The book's epigraph is a quote by British theologian C.S. Lewis from his work titled *Mere Christianity*, which was penned from a collection of BBC radio conversations broadcast between 1941 and 1944.

The following works made their slam debut during my March 2023 feature at Inspired Word's NYC Voices at Parkside Lounge in New York City: "my femininity is that kind of girl," "a woman's place," "the day the moon fell," "Purification in Queens," and "Mother, may I?"

The poem "one can of Canada Dry with a neon pink straw" is dedicated to Gammie, my grandmother Shirley who has instilled in me an unshakeable appreciation for secondhand items or, better still, anything that is free. Her strength as Joseph's sole caretaker (see below) for over seven years is a testament to the endurance of a woman with conviction and endless self-sacrificial love.

The poem "coal for Christmas" is dedicated to Papaw, my grandfather Joseph who sadly passed in December 2016 due to Type 2 Diabetes.

The poem "La Cara Norte" is dedicated to Nano, my grandmother Anna who lit El Paso aflame with her passion to see women's rights implemented, the unhoused given homes thanks to her construction company, and the disappearance of her husband's medical bills due to her highly successful gambling career.

The poem "gone girl and what would've been her eulogy" was inspired by Warsan Shire's "backwards" and Sylvia Plath's "mad girl's love song."

The poem "despite all things, a profession of faith" was inspired by Abigail Carroll's "Creed."

ACKNOWLEDGMENTS

This collection holds such sensitivity, two closed fists around my convictions and my curiosities. I hope this work leaves you steering conversations you cannot predict and developing friendships with those who disagree with you.

Firstly, a massive thank you to Eric and the entire team at Fernwood Press who years ago saw the breadcrumbs of this collection and decided to go all in off a mere three poems I emailed. I cherish your support and the countless modes of assistance you endured to make this book a reality.

To my Women of Words ladies (Audrey, Charissa, Corinne, Elizabeth, Maddie, Sarah Jane, and Serena), each of you has instilled in me a deeper appreciation for language. I hold such gratitude for your capacity to embody the fullness of love so fiercely and faithfully. You have shown me the path to freedom, the path to being untangled.

A massive shoutout to the artist behind the cover and my creative soulmate, Nathanael Myers, who continues to invigorate my quest for bringing banned conversation topics into the dull and drab monotony of small talk. May we continue to live as pioneers in the many intersections of our identities.

My dear Dive and Dine community, thank you for embodying such riveting curiosity into a lived reality during our gatherings. It is a gift to steward such an inquisitive, respectful space with you all.

A warm dose of gratitude to Josh Dunn and the entire CREATIVE.NYC Team at Church of the City who has time and time again advocated and encouraged my Christian faith as the natural genesis for conversation, curiosity, and creative commission.

To my sweet Mom and Dad (if/when you read through these pages), I hope you know how deeply I admire your strength, your shared determination to offer life's best fruit directly into my hungry mouth. These poems exhibit my own nonlinear undertaking to better understand our collective upbringing, who we were, who we are, and what drives us into deeper longing.

To my little blue panda and sister, Ashtin, you have long been my confidante who stirs me into greater joy. Thank you for holding my hand as I wrestle with womanhood, faith, and those damn Maxi pads.

To my beloved, Matt, thank you for listening to each of these poems as I read them to you in dusty subway cars, loud plane cabins, fourteen-hour road trips, or late nights strung out across our bed too tired to pull ourselves between the sheets. Even as I type this, you are doing the laundry to give me this extra hour of writing to finish this book. You are more loyal, more trustworthy, and more loving than I deserve. Thank you for choosing me every day.

To you, dear reader, I hope these pages leave you with a swelling hunger to seek many doors of thought and ask many questions, especially if you have been scorched by religious institutions. Although some of these poems portray a distrust of faith-based organizations or individuals, I firmly believe doubt and questioning are welcomed in the journey of faith. Within my own exploration, I have come to be thoroughly devoted to better understanding the splendor and satiated desire found in God, this Jesus who gives meaning and mercy out to us mortal creatures striding through the world. As C.S. Lewis so brilliantly wrote, "I didn't go to religion to make me happy. I always knew a bottle of Port would do that. If you want a religion to make you feel really comfortable, I certainly don't recommend Christianity."

And again, he describes so emphatically the crux of my wrestling here, "Christianity, if false, is of no importance, and if true, of infinite importance. The only thing it cannot be is moderately important."

ABOUT THE AUTHOR

Kristalyn Gill is a professional human and physical storyteller. Raised in Statesville, North Carolina, she graduated from East Carolina University's Honors College with dual degrees in Dance Performance (BFA) and Interpersonal Communication (BS).

She is the author of the internationally distributed, *The Shape of You* (Free Lines Press, 2021), as well as *The Breakup Club: A Collection of Mishaps and Falling Aparts* (2019). A recipient of the 2023 Queens Arts Fund New Work Grant, she has been celebrated for ushering "shape and movement viscerally across each page in the throes of grief and triumph of girlhood" (Maya Williams, Portland Poet Laureate).

Her writings have been featured in *Dancegeist*, *Dead Dads Club*, *Junk Drawer Magazine* as well as Off-Broadway performances such as *While We Wait* (Candace Brown) and *B_TTERLAND* (Bo Park). She was also a recipient of the 2021 Constance Saltonstall Foundation for the Arts Poetry Fellowship and a featured slam poet at the Bowery Poetry Club, Inspired Word NYC, and Port Veritas.

As a movement artist, Kristalyn has traveled across the globe with credits including Jacob's Pillow Dance Festival, Fire Island

Dance Festival, Solomon R. Guggenheim Museum, and Feud (FX).

Kristalyn currently lives in New York City where she serves as the founder and facilitator of Dive & Dine, a community forum inviting strangers to share a meal and exchange curiosities about culture, faith, and identity.

TITLE INDEX

A
a life worth dying for 103
a list of things that haven't managed to kill me (yet) 113
a man of your word 81
An Ode to my Cervix 50
Ashes and Asics 32
a woman's place 46

B
better, richer, fuller 85
bless your heart, do your part 45

C
casual morbidity 89
clothespin 108
coal for Christmas 76
Confraternity's Resuscitation 21

D
despite all things, a profession of faith 118
drunk on rejection 102

F

food poisoning 107
four valuable lessons from a church-girl 34

G

genu(ine re)flection 22
gone girl and what would've been her eulogy 72

H

have you ever 33
how are you? 106

I

Icarus 109
imago d(e)issent 55
incandescent autumn 110
is this what they call depression? 90
it's not about the nail 30

J

jump 25

L

La Cara Norte 79
little bean 44

M

midnight among the masses 78
Mother, may I? 61
my femininity is that kind of girl 41

N

new age apocrypha 104
nights like these 105

O

one can of Canada Dry with a neon pink straw 68

P

parked in the driveway of a house where I do not live 56
pennies from heaven 35
popcorn prayer circles: a tragedy 36
private school p*ssy 53
pulp fiction 100
purgatory 24
Purification in Queens 31

R

Rosie, just Rosie 48

S

salvation through repetition 91
she only grows near water 70
slipstream 99
slits and ladders 57
speed dial 95
squall—a localized storm, a loud cry 92
supposed thoughtcrimes that leave
    Winston gagging in his sleep 116
surrogacy 80
switchblade 71

T

The All-American Girl is 28 days old 51
the book 12
the burning man 27
the day the moon fell 93
the easter bunny and Jesus 23
the gloaming 49
the great perhaps 17
the hill he dies on 87
the hummingbird and the meadowlark 65
the last, unforgettable line of a nonexistent story 119
the realities of death: an exhaustive list 115

the swan song turned to stone 86
the witches brew 28
too many fathers 82

Y
you are what you eat 18
you can have it all (but not everything) 58

FIRST LINE INDEX

A
Amelia has agreed to go to church with me 36
At 4:00 am, the city's decrescendo 104
a woman's work 48

B
Bad bunny 57

D
Deflowered, lost bloom 92

F
FAITH as in, the epilogue of sun 91
Flying like a bat outta hell 35
Fork sauntering past my cheeks 107

H
Have you ever met a man more story than solid? 81
How do I explain the aftertaste
   of swallowing the whole world 85

I

I am a refugee within my ribs 55
I am fearless with a pair of scissors,
   ready to slaughter 68
I am the alpha, which is to say 109
I am the restless peeling 17
I believe in the importance of dawn 118
I devour the nails and collect the timber 56
If I didn't know any better 34
If the world is your oyster,
   pat that pearl and take a seat 58
I love this park where I can eat
   strawberries in the silence of a 103
In Queens, the mitéra tells the violins to stop playing 46
In the building—the callous, the catalyst—
   known as church 22
In the emergence of summer 99
is me telling you, dear reader 12
I take the priest's homily mouth-to-mouth 21
I think of the saddest story I
   could write, and I think of you 115
It is December, but we are
   not celebrating Jesus' birthday 76
It was then she met God and realized
   her labor and languishing were not in vain 119
I wail for the brutality of missed goodbyes 89

J

Jack be nimble 25
Jesus shotgunning the Father's cup 30

L

Like lavender 106
Little bean burrowing down 44
Little Suz bends so far backward over the sun 49

M

Momma stands a stone's throw across the yard 61
must have a strained relationship 23
My femininity was born and raised 41
my unrequited crush on Diego in 11th grade 113

O

O Great Tongue of Femininity 50
One cup of hibiscus tea 102
On your wedding day 71
Orange like the city, no like the county 100

P

Porcelain palms in protest 95

S

shaved one leg but not the other? 33
Someone will die when it's inconvenient
    for you. You will get 116
Sweet little Anna 79

T

Tardy and a bit tipsy 78
The boy does not yet know he is gentle 87
The day the moon fell, I was asking for an amen 93
the house is a hushed lullaby /
    I know every lyric / by hearth 80
The man burns and is blessed 27
The Maxi pad and the Band-Aid are not friends 51
The mountains have gone copper 110
The night ripens with anticipation 105
The poem begins with the girl opening her eyes 72
There is sand buried in both
    brown Smartwool hiking socks 86
The sidewalk ends in the
    alleyway of my father's teeth 70

The tokophobic has seven
    fallopian tubes in her uterus 45
The woman becomes girl again 18
This borough is the grandmother of red 31
Tongue covered in brass tacks licking up the bullets 65

W

We're late 32
What doesn't kill you brings you to your knees 53
When I used to drive over the I-5 bridge 90
Why should I care to know this intangible,
    merciless, conjectured tyrant of the universe? 82
Witches don't exist, but I know they meet 28

Y

You said you're familiar with dying 24
You smell like California Poppies 108

www.ingramcontent.com/pod-product-compliance
Lightning Source LLC
Chambersburg PA
CBHW011328190426
43193CB00047B/2924